After the eye of the needle had been punched, the head (the part of the needle above the eye) was cleaned up, using a file against a file stop, a block of wood secured to the workbench. The photograph was taken at Shrimpton and Fletcher Ltd, Redditch, in 1927.

NEEDLEMAKING

John G. Rollins
FRGS, MRAI

Shire Publications Ltd

CONTENTS

Published in 2008 by Shire Publications Ltd,
Midland House, West Way, Botley, Oxford
OX2 0PH, UK.
Copyright © 1981 by John G. Rollins. First
published 1981; reprinted 2008 (twice).
Shire Library 71. ISBN 978 0 85263 563 6.

Printed in Great Britain by Ashford Colour Press Ltd, Unit 600, Fareham Reach, Fareham Road,
Gosport, Hants PO13 0FW.

08/1/3

Cover: *John G. Rollins demonstrates needlemaking by hand at his workbench,*

ACKNOWLEDGEMENTS
    The author wishes to thank the principals and staff of the following institutions who have been so
helpful to him in his researches into the history of needlemaking: Dr Paul Craddock, Research
Laboratory, British Museum; British Library, Reference Division; the Bodleian Library;
Buckinghamshire County Records Office; Catholic Records Society; Chester Public Library; City of
Birmingham Central Reference Library; Encyclopaedia Britannica Extension Service; Guildhall
Library, London; Hereford and Worcester County Museum, Hartlebury; Hereford and Worcester
County Records Office; North Yorkshire County Archives; the Public Records Office; Redditch
Borough Council; Redditch Public Library; Science Museum, London; Victoria and Albert Museum,
Department of Textiles; Warwickshire County Museum; Warwickshire County Records Office; West
Sussex Records Office; Wiltshire County Archivist; the Worshipful Company of Needle-makers; and
the York Archaeological Trust. Special thanks are due to Ron Swift, AIIP, ARPS, Department of
Geography, University of Birmingham, who has been responsible for most of the photographic work;
Paddy Parsons, Avoncroft Museum of Buildings, Bromsgrove; John Gilmore, British Needle Com-
pany Ltd, Redditch; Fred Kinchin, Abel Morrall and Company Ltd, Redditch; Bernard Lee, Needle
Industries Ltd, Studley; Horst Lange, Rhein-Nadel Maschinennadel GmbH, Aachen; Universitat-
sbiblotek, Erlangen; Archiv der Stadt Iserlohn; Stadt Koln Historisches Archiv; Archiv der
Hansestadt Lubeck; Stadtbibliothek Nurnberg; Conservatoire National des Arts et Metiers, Paris;
Caisse d'Epargne de L'Aigle, Orne; Monsieur L. Laurent, Syndiest d'Initiative, l'Aigle; Musee Histori-
que des Tissus, Lyon. I must also thank my wife, without whose help and support this work could not
have been completed, Val Homer, for typing the script, and Ray Waring of Alcester Surgical Needle
Company Ltd.
    Illustrations are acknowledged as follows: Ron Swift, cover, pages 3, 7, 9, 10, 11, 14, 26, 27, 30;
Redditch Indicator Company Ltd, page 20; drawn by J. M. Woodward in the 1870s, pages 8 (bottom), 13 (bottom), 18 (top), 22 (bottom), 25 (bottom); from *The Working Man*, 1866, pages 13 (top),
25 (top); author, pages 4, 5, 8 (top), 17, 21, 23, 24; Shrimpton and Fletcher, pages 1, 23; Nurnberg
Standebuch, page 6; *Penny Magazine*, page 24.

In the centre of the photograph is a long-bladed plate clamp holding needles ready for electro-plating. In the foreground needles are shown on a spacing bar before being picked up in the clamp. Some old wooden spacing bars can be seen in the background.

INTRODUCTION

The needle was probably the first tool devised by early man and remains in use today virtually unchanged, although the materials from which it has been made have changed from thorns, through wood, bone and various metals to modern steel alloys, with iron being the most frequently used. Needles were made from meteoric iron, thought to have mystic properties, even before the discovery that iron could be reduced from its ore.

The Romans introduced sophisticated needlemaking into Britain and almost certainly the art of embroidery also. The Saxons, though less skilled, continued to make needles and in time their products equalled those of the Romans. At the time of the Norman conquest of England English embroidery *(Opus Anglicanum)* was famous throughout Europe and much sought after. Although none of the fine needles used in this work survives, the work itself is evidence of their excellence. After the Conquest the skills of the needlemakers were exercised in providing for an expanding range of uses for needles. The seamstress, the tailor, the tentmaker, the sailmaker and the tapestry worker, among others, all required specialised needles. The triangular-pointed needles used by glovers are a good example. Many of the needles we take for granted today were developed during the middle ages. John Stow records that needles were first made in Cheapside, London, during the reign of Queen Mary, by a Moor, who refused to divulge his secrets to anyone, taking them with him to the grave. The only charter granted to a London livery company during the Commonwealth was given to the needlemakers by Oliver Cromwell in 1656 and confirmed by Charles II in 1664.

Where the needles of antiquity no longer survive it is often possible to deduce their type, fineness and construction from a close examination of the work wrought with them. In addition to the everyday uses, needles were applied to a wide variety of art forms, from embroidery to tapestry work, quilting and smocking. These arts have been undertaken by men and women of high and low estate since time immemorial. The enormous range of materials, techniques and styles used by needleworkers throughout the ages illustrates not only the ingenuity of man but also demonstrates that anyone with the time and the patience can produce beautiful, artistic and useful work.

It was once thought that the invention of the sewing machine and modern fabrics would bring about the end of hand sewing. That such was far from the case is demonstrated by the increasing application of modern domestic needlework, while ever greater demands are being made on the needlemaker to supply even more diverse ranges of needles for industry. Consumption of domestic needles throughout the world is the equivalent of roughly three needles per head of population per year.

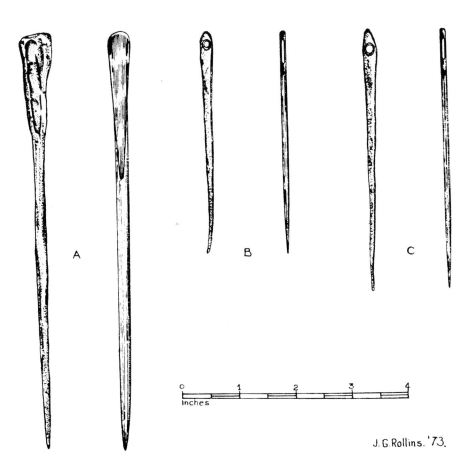

J. G. Rollins. '73.

A comparison of ancient bone needles, probably dating from 1500 BC and found at Buret near Irkutsk in Siberia, with modern counterparts made at Redditch in 1968 shows how little needles have changed: (A) a neolithic awl beside a modern 7-inch (178 mm) upholstery regulator; (B) a bone needle compared with a size 5/0 or 14 double long darner; (C) an antler bone needle with a 4½ inch (114 mm) heavy duty bookbinder's needle.

Seventeenth-century needlemakers' houses by the Salt Way, Feckenham, Worcestershire.

HISTORY OF IRON NEEDLEMAKING IN ENGLAND

During the dark and middle ages most needles were made by specialist needle smiths, who might be whitesmiths also. Some highly skilled blacksmiths, however, may have been capable of producing fine needles and possibly did so from time to time, and coarse needles used for sewing up sacks and similar work were undoubtedly the product of the village or estate smith.

Although iron ores occur frequently in Britain, not all iron is suitable for the manufacture of needles, which requires iron that is malleable and pliable to work and hard and flexible in the finished needle. The best iron was reduced from hematite, an oxide of iron, normally reddish brown in colour, but in some deposits almost black. The Romans worked the hematite ores in the Forest of Dean. The needlemakers in southern England probably obtained their supplies from the Weald of Kent and Sussex, which also supplied the needs of the London needlemakers, even though the iron from the Forest of Dean was superior for the purpose.

Needlemaking developed early in the valley between the Forests of Arden and Feckenham in central England. The Romans worked iron in their settlement at Alcester, on the river Arrow at its con-

5

'The Needlemaker', an illustration by Jost Amman from 'The Standebuch' or Book of Trades (1568). The needlemaker is described as cutting lengths of iron wire for the needles, making the eyes and filing the points.

fluence with the Alne. Saxons occupied the township after the departure of the Romans and continued ironworking there, and Alcester was referred to as a town of smiths in AD 1000. In 1067 the Norman lord, Urse de Abitôt, settled in the valley with his followers, who included some needlemakers, and they may have found others already at work there. In any event, the area later came to be known as the Midland Needle Region.

Cistercian monks established an abbey in 1136 in the river marshes at Bordesley on land donated by King Stephen and the first Earl of Worcester, Waleran de Beaumont, grandson of Urse de Abitôt. They encouraged the craftsmanship and skills of the people in the neighbourhood and are credited with being the true precursors of the local industry. The township of Redditch, which grew up outside the abbey gatehouse, was established as early as 1190.

How and why some of the other needlemaking centres became established is even more difficult to ascertain. London, as England's main port and administrative centre, was able to support highly skilled specialist artisans to supply the needs of the city and its merchants, including clothiers, tailors, sailmakers and cordwainers. The Hanseatic League imported needles into England from Europe and even employed German needlemakers in London. Merchants from Cologne and Lübeck were included in the league; both cities were centres of needle manufacture and continued to dominate the English market until 1563, when the Importation Act stopped the trade, although the manufacture of needles by German craftsmen in

England continued. Christopher Kings, a needlemaker from Cologne, left the Steel Yard near London Bridge in 1559 and set up in the new suburb of Whitechapel. Elias Kuause, another German needlemaker, from Aachen, had established himself on London Bridge by 1566. Needlemakers seem to have shown a predilection for river bridges on which to live and practise their trade, probably because of the quantity of traffic using them and the trading opportunities generated. Needlemakers occupied premises on bridges at Bristol, Chester, Limerick and other places.

There were needlemaking communities in such places as Chichester, Wilton (listed as the chief centre of needlemaking in England in 1250) and York. That at Long Crendon (Buckinghamshire) was established by London needlemakers seeking relief from guild restrictions in 1560 but there may have been earlier needlemaking here, possibly under the patronage of the Augustinian monks of Notley. The needlemakers of Melrose in Scotland had such monastic support. Later centres such as Much Wenlock, Bridgnorth, Chester, Manchester and Hathersage were propagated from existing centres, mostly without lasting success.

A needlemaker's work block.

COTTAGE NEEDLEMAKING

Steel was little used before Tudor times, being considered too hard to work. It was scarce and very variable in quality. Good malleable iron was the best obtainable material for the needlemaker. Needles were made in the artisan's own cottage or in a hovel nearby known as a *pingle*. The needlemaker carried out all the operations of needlemaking himself, assisted at times by members of his family, apprentices and, if he was successful, journeymen assistants.

The needle wire was first cut from flat sheets of iron. Having a square section, the wire had to be rounded by hammering and then *brading* (rubbing down) with sand and water on a cloth. The resultant wire was then cut to the desired length and either pointed or eyed at one end. Some needlemakers preferred to eye the needle first while others pointed their wires before proceeding with the other tasks.

There were two main ways of making the eye. The simplest, and perhaps the oldest, was to flatten the end of the wire and then to split it with a small cold chisel. The bifurcated ends were then splayed out around a form (usually wire of thinner section), the ends closed and hammer-welded to form the eye. Needles of this type were known as *Y-eyed*.

The other method was to punch the eye. This was done using very delicate punches. First, one end of the wire was flattened as previously described. The flattened end was placed on a small anvil mounted in a stout wooden bench known as the *work block*. The *first eying punch* was used to make the impression of the eye in the centre of one of the flat sides, being struck with a small hammer. The wire was then turned over and the operation repeated. In this way the shape of the eye was formed on both sides

7

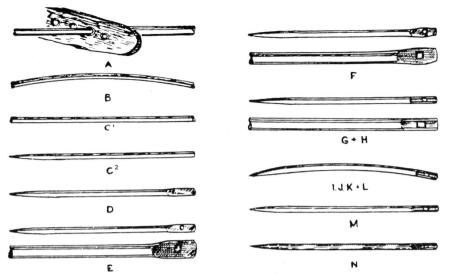

The sequence of operations in needlemaking by hand. (A) The iron wire was drawn down from forged bar and reduced to the required thickness. (B) It was cut into single needle lengths. (C) These, being curved, had to be heated and straightened and then, while still soft, pointed at one end. (D) The opposite ends were flattened on an anvil by hammering, producing two parallel faces. (E) The impression of the eye was made on both faces, leaving a thin membrane. (F) The membrane was punched out on a block of lead, using a delicate punch. (G) Still impaled on the eying punch, or on an eye form, the needle was laid on its side on the anvil and the cheeks were tapped up to form the gutter or thread channel. (H) The gutter was cleaned out with a guttering iron. (I) The needles had to be converted from iron to high carbon steel, known as pieing. (J, K) They were then hardened and tempered. (L) Many needles hardened by being quenched in water when red-hot became distorted and had to be straightened. (M) The needles were scoured clean and polished. (N) After final inspection they were ready for sale.

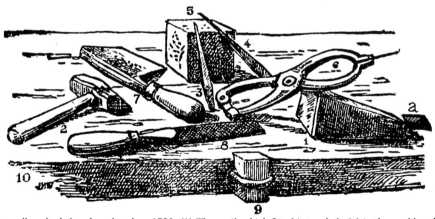

A needlemaker's bench and tools, c 1790. (1) The anvil, which fitted into a hole (a) in the workbench. (2) Flatting hammer; different sizes were used according to the size of needles being made. (3) First eying punch, used to make the impression of the eye. (4) Second eying punch, used to remove the membrane of metal remaining in the eye. (5) Lead block, used to protect the second eying punch in use. (6) Beak-nosed clambs held the needle while work was done around the eye. (7) Guttering iron, for cleaning out the gutter. (8) File; many different ones were used. (9) Filing stop, a wooden block affixed by an iron staple (b) to the front of the bench; the work to be filed was held against it. (10) The work block or bench, made of elm.

8

of the wire, leaving a very thin membrane of metal in the eye. This was removed by using the *second eying punch*. For this operation the wire was removed from the anvil to a small lead block where the remaining metal was punched out. The use of the lead block was solely to protect the delicate second eying punch from damage.

While still impaled on the punch, the needle was taken back to the anvil in order to have the sides of the *gutter* (the thread channel) tapped up. This was a very delicate operation, which freed the punch at the same time. The gutter was finally cleaned out using a special file known as a *guttering iron* and resembling a butcher's cleaver, with the exception that in place of the cutting edge it was provided with a saw-toothed file. The needlemaker equipped himself with several sets of tools according to the size and type of needles to be made. Hammers and guttering irons were referred to by weight expressed in ounces.

In both cases the *head* of the needle above the eye was cleaned up using a file against a *file stop*. The size of the file was again regulated by the type of work in hand. The file stop was a block of wood, usually pear, hawthorn or boxwood, secured to the face of the work block with a wrought iron staple. The file block was used end-grain up, to protect the files from undue wear.

Pointing was done with a file against the file stop. The wire, either *holed* (that is with the eye made) or not, was held in small pliers or pincers fitted with a link-locking device at the end of the handles. These were known as *clambs* (clamps) or, because of their peculiar shape, *beak-nosed clambs*. If the finished point was other than round, it had first to be filed to a round point and afterwards hammered into a flat, triangular or chisel shape.

The making of the needle was now complete except for the removal of the imperfections sustained during manufacture (*work marks*) and polishing. This laborious task was usually undertaken in a variety of ways by the womenfolk and children of the needlemaker. The most efficacious method, however, was found to be *scouring*. For this process the needles were bound up into firm bundles and placed in a leather bag, together with abrasive pebbles, the whole packed as tightly as possible and firmly secured on the outside with thongs to make a roll or bundle. The roll or bundle was placed under a heavy elm board or flagstone and propelled backwards and forwards by the feet of the needlemaker as he worked at his bench. In time the abrasive stones used in the scouring became worn into slender spinules. These were highly prized and carefully preserved by the needlemakers. Some are still found near old scouring sites.

Although needlemaking was considered a very arduous trade, women and girls took part in it. The widow of Adrian Rolyns took over his trade when he died in London in 1547. One of the bogeyman threats used to frighten children was to tell them that they would be put (apprenticed) to needlemaking. Princess Elizabeth, the second daughter of King Charles I, was threatened by her Puritan jailers with such an apprenticeship when she was imprisoned in Carisbrooke Castle the year after her father's execution, and this threat is thought to have been the cause of the depression and subsequent fever from which she died in 1650, when she was only fifteen.

Filing the head of the needle. The needle is held by beak-nosed clambs against the wooden file stop, secured to the edge of the work block.

This was possibly the last operational coal-fired needle-hardening shop in Britain. Work ceased in 1976 and the property was demolished in 1978.

STEEL NEEDLES

In the fifteenth and sixteenth centuries many skilled craftsmen were forced to leave their native countries for religious and political reasons.

The Spanish needlemakers were among these craftsmen, driven from their homeland. They knew the secrets of the Arab method of making steel needles. Spanish steel needles, known in England as *Sprior* needles, were highly prized. The first comedy ever to be written in England was about the loss of a 'goodly Sprior needle', in which an entire village was turned upside down in the search for it. The play was entitled *Gammer Gurton's Needle* and published by Thomas Colwell in 1575. Some of the evicted Spanish needlemakers sought refuge in France and Germany; others found their way into the various English needlemaking communities, where they became known as 'Moor', a reference to their swarthy complexion. Two families of Moors were established in Redditch shortly before the dissolution of the abbey

in 1538, and soon afterwards there were families of Moors living and working as needlemakers in Broad Green and Feckenham as well.

The great failing of wrought iron needles was that they could only be hammered to a certain degree of hardness. Needles made of steel, on the other hand, were hard and resilient. They had a much longer life, were less prone to breakage and did not distort.

Steel is a very difficult material to work up into needles, whereas wrought iron was relatively easier. The ideal was to make needles in wrought iron and then to convert them to steel afterwards, and this was the Spanish method. It was known as *pieing*. The needles were made as before but, when finished, were subjected to the steeling process. For this a hole had to be excavated in the work floor and lined with fireclay or firebricks. When this was done, a fire was set and kept at white heat until the surrounds were white-hot. In the meantime a fireclay crucible had been prepared, with a layer of charcoal in the bottom and then alternate layers of charcoal and needles, until the pot was full. The last layer was again charcoal under a stopping of clay.

When all was ready, the fire was removed from the hole and the crucible placed in it. The hot gleeds were then raked back over it and maintained at white heat for a further twenty-four hours. It was left undisturbed to cool for ten to fourteen days afterwards before being removed from the hole and opened. When removed from the crucible, the needles were found to have absorbed a quantity of carbon from the charcoal, converting the iron to low carbon steel.

Unfortunately the needles had become deformed by excrescences adhering to them and these had to be removed. This was usually done by harsh scouring. The steel needles could then be brought to a desired state of pliability and resilience by *hardening* and *tempering*. To harden the needles they were heated 'cherry' red and then quickly cooled by quenching in water, a process that rendered them hard but very brittle. To restore them to a resilient state it was necessary to reheat and allow them to cool naturally. The needles were then scoured and polished to make them ready for sale.

Steel needles required very prolonged periods of scouring and this could no longer be carried out in the old way under foot. It became the practice to place two bundles of needles (known as a *sett*) on a stout table, over which was placed a heavy elm board, fitted with upright pegs at both ends. Children were employed to push the board (known as a *runner*) backwards and forwards, rotating the sett of bundles underneath. Sand or powdered stone, mixed with water or oil, replaced the stone spinules previously used.

For the final polish (known as the *glaze*) pumice powder, powdered marble or calcined quartzite ground to a fine dust was used. The work was very strenuous and heavy and found to have a harmful effect on the health of the young workers. To counter this, a machine was devised whereby a frame, not unlike a garden gate, was suspended from a beam above and connected to the runner by a wooden rod (usually of ash). This device was found to be much more efficient and easier to work

and became known as a *whee-wah*, from the noise made by the dry hooks and band type of hinges used to support the 'gate'. Until comparatively recent times local children, unable to stand still, were chidden by their parents and told not to 'whee-wah' about. Towards the end of the seventeenth century horse gins were used in the Midlands but were never found to be entirely satisfactory.

Queen Elizabeth I, realising that her realm was technologically backward, covertly encouraged her nobles to install foreign craftsmen on their estates. She did not want these foreign artisans set up in London, where their activities could be monitored by their own ambassadors, but preferred that they should work quietly in the provinces, alongside native craftsmen, who could then learn from them.

Sir Nicholas Throckmorton, the Queen's agent at the French court, persuaded a number of Norman needlemaking families to settle on his family estate at Coughton in Warwickshire. Among them were the Alcocks, Blundles, Chatterleys, Hewitts and Rawlings (Rollins). All were Roman Catholics and one of their number, the Blessed Alexander Rawlings, born in Warwickshire, returned to France to become a secular priest but was apprehended within days of his return to England and burned at the stake in York on 7th April 1595. He was only twenty-one years old when he died.

These people introduced a great innovation to the craft — specialisation. Instead of a single needlemaker being responsible for the whole production of the needle from beginning to end, each man specialised in one process only: wire drawing, pointing, holing (eying), pieing, hardening and tempering (the last three were usually undertaken by the same family) and so on. The cottages they occupied are still standing in Coughton, the property of the Crown. These are two-roomed terrace cottages, with one room upstairs and one downstairs. At the side of the inglenook fireplace on the ground floor of each are to be found small hatches known as *needle hatches,* giving access to the next cottage. As the work progressed, the *dabs* of needles, as they were called, passed from hand to hand down the line: wire came in at one end of the row and finished needles went out at the other.

ABOVE: *The skills of the needle hardener were of prime importance to the needlemaker as the flexibility of the finished needles depended on them. This illustration, from 'The Working Man' published in 1866, shows Jock Pearson working in Richard Turner's hardening shop at Redditch.*

RIGHT: *The scouring shop, drawn by J. M. Woodward (1872), showing needles made up into bundles ('setts') ready for scouring. The knife, twine and heavy hessian cloth were used to make up the bundles. The basket contains pebbles which were ground up and used with the whale oil in the can as the scouring paste. The barrel held water used for washing the scoured needles.*

13

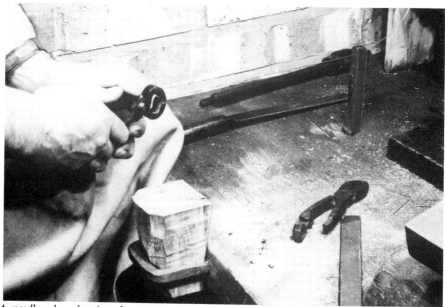

A needlemaker drawing the wire to the required needle size. The wire was delivered to the needlemaker drawn down to Pack size (0.072 inches diameter). The smaller sizes required were drawn by the needlemaker himself.

WATER POWER

Water power had been known and used since Roman times, and almost every reasonable head of water in Britain had already been harnessed to power grist mills, flax mills, fulling stocks, tucking mills and the like, but its application to the more laborious processes of the metalworking trades had to wait until the mid sixteenth century.

The drawing of iron wire was the first of the processes affecting needlemaking to which water power was applied. Previously all wire drawn in Britain had been drawn by hand. The continentals, using water-powered machinery, produced uniform wire much earlier, their more malleable products being preferred by English needlemakers to the rough and inconsistent local wire. The Cistercian monks of Tintern had always encouraged the drawing of iron wire on their estates in the Forest of Dean. Following the dissolution of the monasteries, however, the industry went into a serious recession. The highly skilled hammermen employed by the monks were discharged and cheaper labour was employed, resulting in an inevitable loss of skills. As late as 1596 complaints were still being made in London concerning 'the badness of the iron and the bad workmanship of the wire drawers'. Following the Elizabethan practice, twenty-two German wire drawers and their families under the leadership of Christopher Shültz were brought to Tintern in 1565. A water-powered wire-drawing mill was built in the Angidy valley on ground belonging to the Earl of Worcester. A report on 7th November 1566 stated that 'The artificial house for wire is in good forwardness; which house contains about 50 feet in length and 30 in breadth. In the same cometh as many works as 4 (water) wheels can drive, also 2 furnaces for annealing and 2 forges.'

The optimism reflected in this report was

not justified, however, with the result that the mill, when it finally became available, was rented to a partnership comprising John Wheler and Andrew Palmer. John Wheler died in 1575 before the enterprise could be made viable and his widow sold her share to Richard Hanbury. The Hanbury family had been the overseers of the monastic metalworkers of Bordesley Abbey in Worcestershire before the dissolution in 1538, shortly after which Richard's father had removed his entire family to Elmley Lovett, where John Wheler also lived. Richard was well qualified to take on the oversight of a wire mill as he was already concerned with the production of 'Osmond' iron in the Forest. *Osmond* was the name given to the ductile iron reduced from the haematic ores mined in the Forest of Dean. The name was a corruption of the Swedish *Orr grund* iron, of which it was considered almost the equal. Hanbury would have had previous experience of wire drawing from his childhood in the Forest of Feckenham.

Before the introduction of water power only four sizes of wire were produced. They were named *Middling, Great Boultock, Small Boultock* and *Buckling,* and the needlemakers themselves made any further reductions. Only four sizes of needles were produced in a variety of lengths at that time, with specialised points for cordwainers, glovers, saddlers and the like. Surgeons used glovers' needles to suture the wounds of their patients.

The introduction of water power resulted in a much smoother and more uniform wire and the range of sizes was increased to twelve, now known as *Rip* (the same as Middling), *Great Boultock, Small Boultock, Slip, Buckle, Two Band, Riving, Northern* (produced specifically to meet the needs of the Midland and Welsh needlemakers living on the northern reaches of the river Severn), *Clarvant, Bastard, Fine* and *Fine Fine.*

Randle Holme, writing in 1688 in the *Academy of Armour,* lists the range of needles available at that time as *Buth Lane,* the largest (a special needle), and, in descending order of size, needles numbered 1 to 10, culminating with another special needle known as a *Pearl* (later the largest size of bead needle). There was then a great vogue for pearl adornments on clothes and

this fine needle was produced to meet that demand. He also mentions glovers' needles (with square points), bookbinders' needles (with long round points), sow-gelders' needles (with flat points), chyrurgions' (surgeons') needles (with triangular points) and pack needles (some flat and some crooked at the point), demonstrating the increased demand for needles and the degree of specialisation that was the needlemakers' response to that demand.

Skilled needlemakers have always tried to improve the quality and range of the needles they made. The story is told of one master needlemaker, Charles Rawlings (1718-99) of Alcester, who had striven all his working life to make a near perfect set of sewing needles. Try as he would, he was always defeated by some flaw that rendered his needles less than perfect by his own high standard. As the years passed in unremitting labour he was rewarded by one near perfect needle and months or years later by another, until at last he had the complete range, highly polished, strong and resilient, with perfectly formed sharp points and smooth eyes. He kept them secretly, carefully stored in a wash-leather wallet, showing them to no one. They were, and remained, the standard by which he judged all other work. He was admitted a free brother of the Worshipful Company of Needlemakers in 1781. When at the end of his working life he retired to Dorsington, near Stratford upon Avon, he took his test set with him. Occasionally he would take them out of their case and admire them. One day he detected small specks of rust marring their perfection. Only then did he show the set to his son, before destroying them. When asked why he had kept them secret, the old man replied: 'Had I shown this set to anyone, all my customers would have demanded needles of the same quality. It took me years to make such needles as these. For me to make a living would have been impossible. I should have been unable to sell even the commoner sorts of needles.'

The London needlemakers developed a water-driven machine for pointing needles. These machines were so dangerous to operate that in 1623 a complaint was made against their use to the Privy Council, resulting in their ruthless suppression. One such machine was broken up in 1629 and

Needle (wire) sizes

Name	diameter (inches)	sewing needle size numbers	sharps	carpet sharps	betweens	straws	crewel or embroidery	darners or (L) large darners	tapestry or rug	lo-lo or bead	knitting
000 Nail (or Five Shilling) Bar	0.372										
00 Rip (Middle Cut or Middling)	0.348										
0 Great (or Heavy) Boultock	0.324										
1 Small (or Light) Boultock	0.300										1
2 Buckling (Buckle)	0.276										2
3 Large Raven	0.252										3
4 Middle Raven	0.232										4
5 Small Middle Raven	0.212										5
6 Small Raven (or Cleven)	0.192										6
7 Clarvant	0.176										7
8 Bastard (or Coarse Fine)	0.160										8
9 Fine	0.144										9
10 Super Fine	0.128										10
11 Fine Fine	0.116										11
12 Needle (or Northern)	0.104							12(L)			12
13 Middle Needle (or Great Pack)	0.092							13(L)			13
14 Small Needle (or Middle Pack)	0.080							14(L)	14		14
15 Pack (or Pack Thread)	0.072							15(L)	15		15
16 One Band (First Pass)	0.064	0/3		3/0				16(L)	16		16
17 Two Band	0.056	0/2		2/0				17(L)	17		17
18 Three Band	0.050	0/1*		1/0				18(L)	18		18
19 Four Band	0.046	1	1	1	1	1	1	1	19		19
20 Five Band	0.043	2	2	2	2	2	2	2	20		20
21 Six Band	0.040	3	3	3	3	3	3	3	21		21
22 Seven Band	0.037	4	4	4	4	4	4	4	22		
23 Eight Band	0.034	5	5	5	5	5	5	5	23		
24 Nine Band	0.030	6	6	6	6	6	6	6	24		
25 Ten Band	0.027	7	7	7	7	7	7	7	25		
26 Eleven Band	0.024	8	8	8	8	8	8	8			
27 Twelve Band	0.021	9	9	9	9	9	9	9			
28	0.018	10	10			10	10				
29	0.016	11	11				11			11	
		(pearl)									
30	0.014	12S	12							1/12	
31	0.013	13S								2/13	
32	0.012	14S								3/14	
33	0.010	15S								4/15	
34	0.009	16S								5/16	
35	0.008	17S									

*Buth Lane 1688

Note: These sizes remained in use until 1976, when metric wire sizes were adopted. It is impossible to include in this list the whole range of needles, domestic, surgical, industrial, sewing machine etc, but it gives some idea of the range of diameters, each of which is available in a variety of lengths.

the needlemaker was arrested.

Lord Windsor, whose family had been granted the Bordesley Abbey lands in 1542, died in 1722. He had ironworking interests in South Wales and the Forest of Dean as well as furnaces and forges in the Arrow valley in Worcestershire. At the time of his death the British iron trade was in a depressed state. His successor disposed of his South Welsh and Forest of Dean interests but could find no market or tenants for the Arrow valley mills.

Eventually the Forge Mills at Redditch were let to the needlemaking Chillingworth family some time before 1730. It is almost certain that wire drawing for the local needle trade was being undertaken at Forge Mills at the time and that the Chillingworths took over the mills in order to secure their supplies of wire.

The next great development in the needle trade was the application of water power to the very heavy process of needle scouring. Three mills were in use down the valley by 1730, Forge Mills at Redditch, Washford Mill at Studley and Sambourne Mill. The Forge Mills at Redditch were the last to operate. The final dab of needles was scoured there by Harry Jakeman on 2nd May 1958.

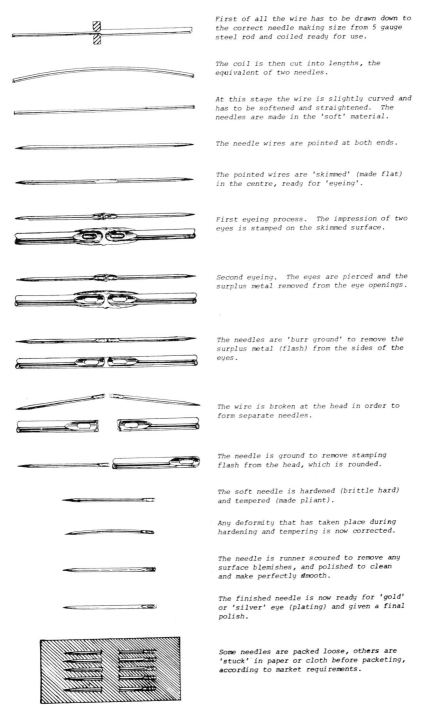

First of all the wire has to be drawn down to the correct needle making size from 5 gauge steel rod and coiled ready for use.

The coil is then cut into lengths, the equivalent of two needles.

At this stage the wire is slightly curved and has to be softened and straightened. The needles are made in the 'soft' material.

The needle wires are pointed at both ends.

The pointed wires are 'skimmed' (made flat) in the centre, ready for 'eyeing'.

First eyeing process. The impression of two eyes is stamped on the skimmed surface.

Second eyeing. The eyes are pierced and the surplus metal removed from the eye openings.

The needles are 'burr ground' to remove the surplus metal (flash) from the sides of the eyes.

The wire is broken at the head in order to form separate needles.

The needle is ground to remove stamping flash from the head, which is rounded.

The soft needle is hardened (brittle hard) and tempered (made pliant).

Any deformity that has taken place during hardening and tempering is now corrected.

The needle is runner scoured to remove any surface blemishes, and polished to clean and make perfectly smooth.

The finished needle is now ready for 'gold' or 'silver' eye (plating) and given a final polish.

Some needles are packed loose, others are 'stuck' in paper or cloth before packeting, according to market requirements.

The various processes in the manufacture of steel needles.

ABOVE: *The needle hardener's rubbing tools: (1) rubbing rings with (2) needle wires; (3) straightening tool (soft file); (4) a pair of 'duck foot' trowels, used to regulate the hot wires; (5) pincers or pliers; (6) rubbing rings (the size of the rings used varied according to the size of wire to be straightened); (7) a double soft file with slots in which the rings fitted; (8) hardening plate of cast iron.*

RIGHT: *Rubbing was the first process after the needle wires had been cut to length. The wires were all misformed at this stage and had to be straightened. This was done by heating them 'cherry red', held between two rings, and rubbing them with a tool known as a soft file until straight.*

The staff and workpeople of Kirby Beard and Company on the eve of their move from Long Crendon, Buckinghamshire, to Redditch in 1862. Two-thirds of the work force moved with the company to find new homes in Redditch.

THE CONCENTRATION OF NEEDLEMAKING AT REDDITCH

The application of water power to the heavy and laborious process of needle scouring by the Redditch needlemakers was the great advance that culminated in the acceptance of Redditch needles as the best in the world. Needles made by hand suffered many blemishes during the manufacturing processes, all of which had to be removed before the needles could be sold. In order to do this the needles were packed in tight bundles called *setts* in heavy sackcloth, *hessian, hurden* or *burlap* being names of various grades of heavy hemp and jute cloth so used. The squares of cloth, cut to size, were placed in several layers in a special wooden trough about 20 inches (500 mm) long. The needles were then placed lengthwise on the cloth in the trough, about 65,000 needles to a sett, according to size. In the old days of handwork two bundles were referred to as a sett but with the advent of water power the term was applied to a single bundle only. Train oil, soap suds or in some cases clay slurry was poured over the needles and emery powder (as the powdered local quartz was termed) was spread over them. True emery or corundum from the Greek island of Naxos was not used in the needle trade before 1912. End patches were inserted to prevent the needles 'working' and the bundle was rolled up as tightly as possible and secured with strong twine or thread. In order to be able to exert the maximum pressure during the tying up the scourer made use of an upright post secured to the benchend, known as a *tie horse*. Once the sett had been secured holes were made in it and more oil or suds inserted. A can with a long spout, known as a *sud spot*, was used. The setts were then placed two under each runner and subjected to continuous rolling for about eight hours, known as a *scour*.

The needles were then removed from the sett and washed clean in hot water, in dou-

The lower scouring shop at Forge Mills, Redditch, which were probably the first watermills to have been adapted for a needlemaking process — needle scouring. The last needles were scoured at the mills on 2nd May 1958.

ble open boilers called *coppers* (even though they were usually cast iron after about 1810). The needles were placed in very fine sieves to be washed, first in the dirty side and then in the clean side of the copper. Afterwards they were dried in revolving barrels in hot dry bran or sawdust. The needles were then repacked in the same grade of emery and subjected to a further eight hours under the runners. This sequence was repeated four times (eight scours), using different grades of emery. Finally two polishes were undertaken, known as the *glaze,* using putty (oxide of tin) or pumice powder and olive oil. When the needles were thoroughly dried they had to be separated from the drying materials. This was accomplished with a *fanning-out tray* (a reference to the earlier method when the bran was actually removed by fanning), in which the needles were skilfully shaken to effect separation.

Scouring mills operated continuously throughout the twenty-four hours as long as water was available. During the winter frost and ice were often an impediment. In the summer long droughts also forced the scourers to 'tread the wheel' for weeks or even months at a time. On large wheels, like the ones at Forge Mills, Redditch, and Beoley Mill, four men at a time would walk the wheel like a treadmill. They trod for fifteen minutes, after which the end man would step off. The other three moved over one place and a new man filled the gap at the other end. In this way each man worked for one hour and rested for fifteen minutes.

Normally scourers worked twelve-hour shifts from after evensong on Sunday until six o'clock on Saturday evening. The west wing of the Forge Mills, which was a two-bed mill (it had two scouring shops, one up and one down, known as the upper and

20

lower beds respectively, each with sixteen runners), was manned by five men and two boys during the day and two men and one boy at night. The boys were used to fetch and carry for the scourers, while at the same time learning the trade.

Eight scours and two polishes constituted a week's work, about four million needles. The finish of the needles that emerged from this long process was of such high quality that other needlemaking communities not equipped with water-powered scouring mills were unable to compete either in quality or price. The result was that needlemakers began to drift into the Midland needlemaking region from all over Britain. The first community to move was the Welsh needlemakers in 1790.

The *Directory of England and Wales* for that year gave Alcester as the chief seat of needle manufacture but it was soon displaced by Studley and by 1850 the accolade had passed to Redditch, where over 2,500 men, women and children were employed in the district to produce over 200 million needles each year.

Early in the nineteenth century the Long Crendon needlemakers became disturbed by the competition they were experiencing and dispatched an emissary, Jonas Shrimpton, to the Midlands to assess the situation. There is little evidence that he ever travelled beyond Alcester, but his report, when he returned, was so alarming that the trickle of emigrating needlemakers soon became a flood. Not all the people who came into the

The barrelling shop at Forge Mills, Redditch. After scouring, the needles were washed and then placed in revolving barrels with warm bran or sawdust in order to dry them.

The flypress, used for second eying, was introduced into the Redditch needle trade in 1798. First developed by the French and used at the Paris mint as early as 1552, flypresses were introduced to the Royal Mint in the Tower of London in 1662. They were installed at Matthew Boulton's new factory in Soho, Birmingham, in 1763 and quickly adopted by other Birmingham manufacturers.

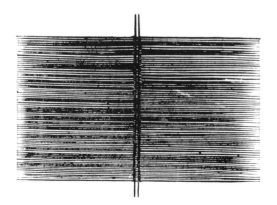

Needles spitted for head filing. When the needles had been eyed they were threaded on to wires for the filer, who then removed the surplus metal from around the eyes. When this operation had been completed he would separate the needles and file the heads round.

The needle stamping shop at Shrimpton and Fletcher Ltd, Queen Street, Redditch, in 1927. The factory has since been demolished.

district were needlemakers. Other skills were needed in the rapidly expanding community. Allied trades such as filemakers, bellows makers and wire drawers, builders, carpenters and farmers also came.

On Sunday 28th January 1844 one such group left Long Crendon at midnight for Astwood Bank after a farewell party and tearful goodbyes. Led by John Shrimpton, the party consisted of his wife and three children, his apprentice William Hawkes, Ephraim Harris, his wife and two children, John Solomon Shrimpton with his wife and child and young Solomon David Shrimpton. A farmer, John Kirby Shrimpton, provided a covered wagon and two horses, in which the women and children travelled, and another farmer, William Carter, provided a covered wagon and four horses to convey their household effects, stock in trade and tools. Driver William Towersey accompanied the two horses and wagon while Driver Ernie Beckett was responsible for the four-horse team. The route they followed was by way of Bicester, Banbury, Edge Hill, Stratford upon Avon and Alcester to Astwood Bank. They halted at night at wayside inns, the women and children being accommodated in the inns, the men sleeping in the wagons. The journey took three days, arriving at two o'clock in the morning on 1st February. William Carter continued as a farmer in his new home and died in Tardebigge parish aged 110. The last firm to move from Long Crendon to Redditch was Kirby Beard and Company, who made the journey in 1862, by which time Redditch had become the undisputed centre of British needlemaking.

Packmen, when they visited the needle districts, were not always well received, especially if they were thought to be peddling 'foreign' needles (any needles other than strictly local ones). Such itinerant traders, when they called at the needle mills, were usually induced to open their packs outside one of the lower beds (as the scouring shops were known) and then, while their attention was momentarily distracted, would have a bucket of 'dotment' (the warm residue taken from the dirty side of the washing boiler) emptied over them from

23

Needle pointing on water-powered dry stones was introduced into the trade about 1780. It was very injurious to health and few pointers lived to beyond their thirtieth birthday. Yet they resisted all attempts to better their working conditions, even striking against the implementation of improvements. This drawing of a pointer at work was published in the 'Penny Magazine', January 1843, but is thought to be older.

the upper beds. When the poor fellows remonstrated, the scourers would drag them through the mill pool thus setting the grease, making it almost impossible to remove from their clothing and completely ruining their stock in trade.

Shortly after the Napoleonic Wars, when ships were being paid off, Dr C. Brown, RN, invested what money he had in a pack and tramped the countryside. He came to Studley in 1816 and unfortunately fell foul of the local needlemakers and was given the treatment, as a result of which he lost his pack. Destitute, he decided to remain in Studley. Assisted by the repentant needlemakers, he set up in Marble Alley as a doctor, spending the remainder of his days ministering to the sick in the village and surrounding countryside. A large, somewhat taciturn man, he commanded great respect. He could be seen daily walking considerable distances to visit his patients in Astwood Bank and elsewhere.

The pointing of needles on high-speed power-driven sandstones was introduced into the trade about 1780.

John Mills, who took over the converted Ipsley Mill in 1760, was probably experimenting with the idea as early as 1765, when he was charged threepence for a 'thing for the mill', and in 1766 for warps and stones, and again in 1767 for seven new pointing stones, warps and pulleys. Needles were almost certainly being pointed by dry grinding in 1780.

This 'new' process was almost certainly similar to the one developed by the London needlemakers a hundred years earlier, and just as deadly. The first stones used were pierced with a square hole and fitted tightly on to a square shaft. This was accepted practice for edge grinders at that time, but it was found that at the high speeds required to obtain a good point the stones tended to crack in the corners of the holes under centrifugal force and break-up, caus-

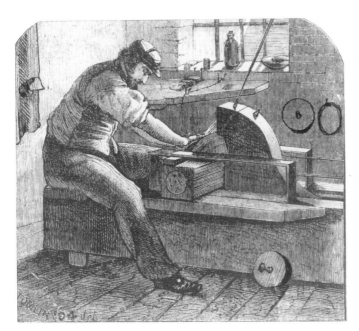

A needle pointer, Bill Tomlinson, at work in Richard Turner's factory in Breedon, Redditch. He is using an exhauster fan, which was introduced to the Redditch pointing mills in 1844. The pointers went on strike against it, staying out for nearly twelve months, but the fan was finally accepted in 1845.

The needle pointing machine was invented and developed by a Redditch man, Colin Banks, but it met with strong opposition in Britain: the Redditch pointers purchased his first machine and ceremoniously smashed it in 1846. Banks took his plans to Germany, where he sold them to the needle manufacturer Schleicher of Schonthal near Aachen. Schleicher's improved machines were afterwards made by Kaiser of Iserlohn.

ing serious injuries and sometimes death. Disturbing as this was, it was not the worst aspect. The dust given off during pointing soon proved to be a killer. The pointers worked in semi-darkness in order to see the points forming by the light of their own sparks. The whole time they were enveloped in clouds of dust. It was found impossible for young men to become pointers until they had matured. The life of a pointer was considered to be about seven years, few surviving to see their thirtieth birthday. They were well paid and refused any improvements in their working conditions for fear that their emoluments would be curtailed. When S. Thomas and Son introduced J. C. Chambers's fan into British mills the pointers went on strike for twelve months. Ultimately a much greater threat was posed by Colin Banks's pointing machine. The pointers purchased the first one from him and ceremoniously smashed it up on the Redditch Church Green in 1854. Colin Banks used the money to go to Aachen, where he sold his invention to the needlemaker Schleicher of Schönthal and set himself up with the proceeds in Iserlohn, selling out to Hermann Joseph Neuss in 1860. He then returned home and built his own factory in Redditch.

Extracts from a poem written in 1840 express the mood of the times:

In hurden aprons and paper caps
   the scourers looked such funny chaps.
Blue-pointers dressed like other men
   for they were thought quite gentlemen.
What wicked men the pointers were
   to drink and curse and fight and swear.
A short and merry life they'd lead
   and of the future take no heed.
Hard times for those who'd work
   twelve hours a day, one couldn't shirk.
The bell was rung and you must hear
   or the 'sack' you'd get first pay day near.
Saturdays brought them no enjoyment
   they stayed till six at their employment.
Boys and girls eight, nine and ten
   Toed the mark with women and men.
Village stampers brought their pockets
   hung in wallets behind their jackets.
With ninety thousand (needles) on heel and toe
   'twas a hardish walk from Crowder's Row (Crabbs Cross).

The last man to make needles by hand was William Bradbury, who, in his last years, lived with his daughter Ann and son-in-law Thomas Morrall in a cottage in Green Lane, Studley. He had a contract with a London house, which they honoured, agreeing to take all the needles he made as long as he lived. William died in 1851 and his tools were sold to Michael T. Morrall. Abel Morrall and Company exhibited them at the Philadelphia Exhibition in 1876. Regrettably, although heavily insured, they were never returned to Britain.

Straightening 'crooks' (bent needles) after hardening and tempering. A soft file (an old file with the cutting surface removed) was used to roll the needles on a heavy iron plate until they were straight.

Setting needle points after scouring. Bill Shakles at work in 1965 in the factory of George Hollington and Sons at Astwood Bank.

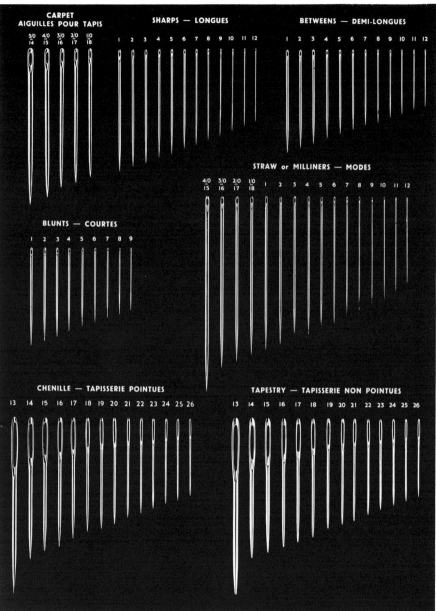

Needle size chart. Sharps are the needles most commonly used in the home for domestic sewing. They are also made in heavier sizes, termed carpet sharps, for repairing rugs and carpets. Betweens and blunts are similar to but shorter than sharps and are favoured by tailors because they can sew more quickly with a short, strong needle and carry out fine work in heavy materials. Straw needles, longer than sharps, are used by milliners and are so called because many hats were made of straw. Chenille needles have very large eyes to take the thick fluffy wools used in some embroidery work and sharp points for embroidering on closely woven materials. Tapestry needles have large eyes but blunt points and are ideal for embroidery or tapestry work on canvas, scrim or net.

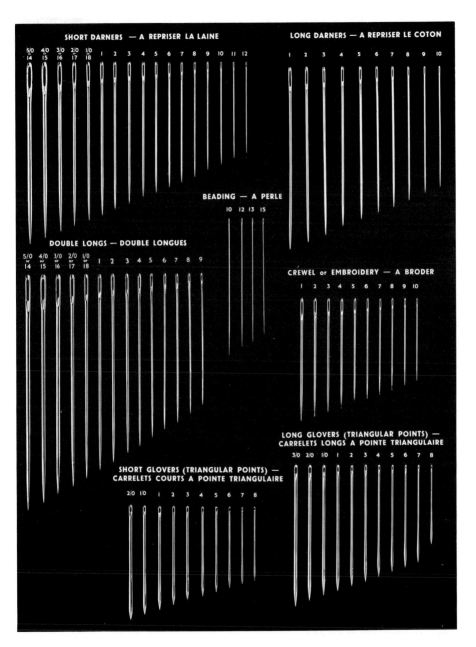

Needle size chart. Darners have large eyes to take the fluffy wools used for darning holes and are longer than sharps in order to reach across a hole and weave in and out round its edges. Double long darners are for mending large holes in thick materials. Crewel needles are the same length and thickness as sharps but have larger eyes to take the flossy silks used in embroidery. Similar to double longs, beading needles are made only in very fine sizes for threading beads and sequins. Glovers are used for glovemaking: their triangular points ensure that the leather is cut, not torn, by the needle.

The polishing shop, Alcester Surgical Needle Company, c 1960. The skills and craftsmanship of the old-time needlemakers have survived in the manufacture of surgical needles longer than in any other branch of the trade, partly because of the great variety of surgical needles produced and the small numbers needed of each type. The polishers' skills are a vital part of surgical needlemaking. Glovers' needles were used until French army surgeons found it expeditious to heat and bend them into semicircular shapes. From then on demand for specialist surgical needles increased steadily. The Long Crendon needlemakers concentrated on surgical needles and took their knowledge with them when they migrated to the Midlands. Emanuel Shrimpton and Thomas Fletcher established themselves in Redditch, which became famous for its surgical needles. Shrimpton and Fletcher and the Alcester Surgical Needle Company are now part of Needle Industries Ltd.

GLOSSARY

Anvil: a small metal work block in a variety of shapes and sizes. Usually set into the work bench.

Barrelling: method of drying needles after they had been washed to remove the scouring compound. The needles were subjected to violent motion in hot sawdust or bran in a revolving barrel.

Beak-nosed clamb: a clamp or pincers used to hold single needles while work was being done on them.

Betweens: a shorter version of *sharps* used by tailors.

Block: the needlemaker's bench or work block.

Canvas embroidery needles: the same range of needles as *chenille* but with larger eyes.

Carpet needles: short thick needles.

Chenille needles: needles with very large eyes and sharp points.

Clamb: a clamp used to hold the needles.

Crewel needles: needles with extra large eyes.

Crooks: needles distorted by quenching after hardening.

Darners: needles used for mending heavy materials.

Double long darners: longer versions of darning needles.

Embroidery needles: the same as *crewel needles*.

Extruded eye: an early method of forming the eye of a needle by forging. The head is extruded into a long thing tang, which is then bent to form the eye and hammer-welded. Used in the making of bronze and iron needles.

Eye: the hole at the head to take the thread.

Eying punch: the punch used to punch the eye in a needle. The first eying punch was used to make the impression of the eye on both sides of the needle. The second eying punch, a very slender tool, was used to punch out the eye.

Eyer: also referred to as a holer. One who makes the eyes in the needle.

Fanning-out tray: a parabolic tray used to separate the needles from the sawdust after barrelling.

Fetler: a filer, usually one who points needles with a file.

Finisher or Furnisher: the person responsi-

ble for the remedial work required to perfect the finished needle.

Guttering iron: a cleaver-like tool with a file edge used to clear the thread channel at the eye.

Handing knife: used to bring all the needles the same way.

Handing and weighing: the process of getting all the needles to point the same way and quantifying them.

Holer: see *eyer*.

Lead: the lead block on which the second eying punch is used to pierce the eye. Lead was used in order not to damage the delicate punch.

Papering: the process of sticking the needles in paper or cloth for sale, also referred to as 'sticking'.

Plate clamb: clamp with wide plate jaws used to hold the needles, a quantity at a time, in order to grind the heads.

Pointer: one who points the needles on a dry grinding stone.

Runner: the upper moving part of a scouring machine.

Runner bed: the table over which the runner moves.

Scourer: the craftsman who does the scouring, a series of cleaning and polishing operations.

Scouring: see *scourer*. In the days of domestic needlemaking and hand scouring two scours and a polish were considered sufficient, but after the application of water power in 1730 as many as eight scours and two polishes were given, each of eight hours duration. This was the secret of the excellence of Redditch-made needles, which became known as the best in the world. Today with better materials one scour and one polish are deemed sufficient.

Sett: the roll or bundle of needles made up to go under the scouring runner. Originally two such bundles comprised a sett; today a single bundle is so called.

Sharps: common sewing needle, used for plain sewing.

Snob: a pointer using a hammer to form the point, usually triangular or chisel.

Soft file: a metal bar used by the hardener to straighten the wires between rings, or the tool used by the soft straightener, so called because they were often made from worn files.

Soft straightener: usually a woman whose occupation it was to straighten the *crooks* caused by quenching in water during the hardening process.

Straws: a longer version of *sharps* needles, used by embroiderers. So called because they were originally made for the Luton straw hat trade.

Sud spot: a can with a long spout used to top up the sett before scouring.

Sweep: the arm operating the scouring runner, usually made of ash or lance wood.

Tapestry needles: similar to *chenille needles* except that their points are blunt.

Wool embroidery: see *chenille needles*.

FURTHER READING

Avery, William. *Old Redditch.* Redditch Indicator Co Ltd, 1887.

Bartleet, Edgar S. *History of a Needle.* Hudson and Sons, Birmingham, 1890.

Dickens, Margaret. *A Thousand Years in Tardebigge.* Cornish Brothers, Birmingham, 1931.

Donald, Joyce. 'The Crendon Needle-makers'. *Records of Buckinghamshire,* volume XIX part 1, 1971.

Guise, H. *Needles.* Redditch Indicator Co Ltd, 1936.

Hayward, L. *Surgical Needles Ancient and Modern.* Institute of British Surgical Technicians, 1961.

Heming, W. T. *The Needle Region and its Resources.* Redditch Indicator Co Ltd, 1877.

Hulme, E. Wyndham. 'Chichester Needles'. *Sussex Notes and Queries,* volume 12, pages 124-5, 1948.

Maury, J. Translated by Arthur Edmunds. *Laungerie Bass Excavations.* Imprinterie Mannoyr, 1925.

Morrall, A. E. *Short Description of Needle-making.* Express Printing, Redditch, 1886.

Morrall, Michael T. *History and Description of Needle Making.* A. Hobson, Ashton-under-Lyne, 1852.

Page, Dr H. *The Sewing Needle.* Redditch Indicator Co Ltd, 1896.

Rogers, E. H. *Stratification of the Cave Earth in Kents Cavern.* Devon Archaeological Exploration Society, 1954.

Rollins, J. G. *Early Victorian Needlemakers 1830-1860.* Costume Society, 1969.

Rollins, J. G. *The Needle Mills.* SPAB number 10, 1970.

Rollins, J. G. *A Short History of Redditch.* Redditch Indicator Co Ltd, 1970.

Rollins, J. G. 'Redditch Forge Mills'. *Archaeological Journal,* volume CXXVII, 1971.

Rollins, J. G. 'Forge Mills, Redditch: From Abbey Metal Works to Museum of the Needlemaking Industry.' *Industrial Archaeology* volume 16 number 2, pages 158-69, 1981.

Shrimpton, William (editor). *Notes on a Decayed Needle-land.* Redditch Indicator Co Ltd, 1897.

Steer, Dr Francis W. *Some Chichester Tradesmen 1652-1836.* Chichester City Council, number 17, 1960.

Steer, Dr Francis W. *The Chichester Needle Industry.* Chichester City Council number 31, 1961.

Timmins, Samuel (editor). *Midland Hardware District,* pages 197-9, 1866. Reprinted Frank Cass and Co Ltd, 1967.

White, George. 'History of Early Needle-making'. *Newcomen Transactions,* volume XXI, 1941.

PLACES TO VISIT

Forge Mill Needle Museum, Needle Mill Lane, Riverside, Redditch, Worcestershire B98 8HY. Telephone: 01527 62509. Website: www.redditch.whub.org.uk

Worcestershire County Museum, Hartlebury Castle, Hartlebury, near Kidderminster, Worcestershire DY11 7XZ. Telephone: 01299 250416. Website: http://worcestershire.whub.org.uk

Most museums have examples of ancient needles, including departments of the British Museum and the Victoria and Albert Museum.